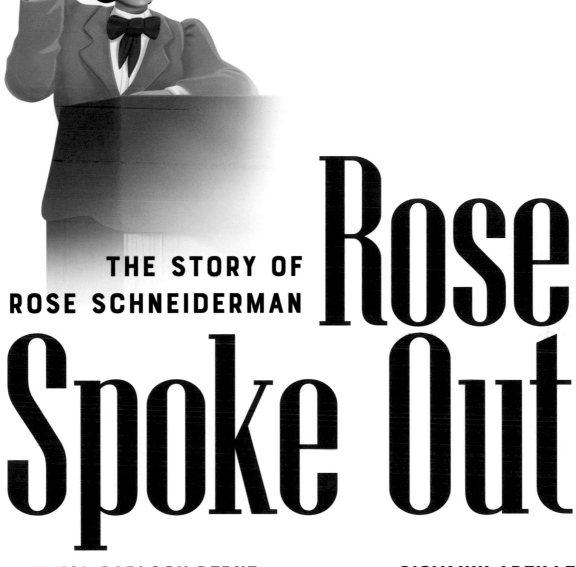

THE STORY OF ROSE SCHNEIDERMAN

Rose Spoke Out

BY **EMMA CARLSON BERNE** · ILLUSTRATED BY **GIOVANNI ABEILLE**

AN IMPRINT OF BEHRMAN HOUSE

www.applesandhoneypress.com

For Oscar—ECB

For Alice—GA

Apples & Honey Press
An imprint of Behrman House
Millburn, New Jersey 07041

www.applesandhoneypress.com

ISBN 978-1-68115-617-0

Library of Congress Cataloging-in-Publication Data

Names: Berne, Emma Carlson, 1979- author. | Abeille, Giovanni, illustrator.

Title: Rose spoke out : the story of Rose Schneiderman / by Emma Carlson
    Berne ; illustrated by Giovanni Abeille.
Description: Millburn, New Jersey : Apples & Honey Press, [2023] |
    Audience: Ages 5-8 | Audience: Grades 2-3 | Summary: "A picture book
    biography of American labor leader Rose Schneiderman"-- Provided by
    publisher.
Identifiers: LCCN 2022030188 | ISBN 9781681156170 (hardback)
Subjects: LCSH: Schneiderman, Rose, 1882-1972. | Labor unions--United
    States--Juvenile literature. | Women--Employment--United
    States--Biography--Juvenile literature.
Classification: LCC HD6079 .B47 2023 | DDC
    331.880920924/eng/20220901--dcundefined
LC record available at https://lccn.loc.gov/2022030188

Design by Zatar Creative
Edited by Aviva Lucas Gutnick
Art Directed by Ann D. Koffsky

Printed in the United States of America

1 3 5 7 9 8 6 4 2

Rose loved school.

She loved studying
and arguing about ideas.
And she talked a *lot*.

Rose's mother said
she had a big mouth.

Rose didn't think so.
She thought she had a
big voice.

Rose used her big voice to help too.

Once, when her little brother Harry couldn't ask the Four Questions at the Passover seder, Rose spoke the Hebrew words for him.

Then Rose's father died.

Her mother scrubbed floors and cleaned to support the family.

But she couldn't earn enough money.

Rose had to leave school and go to work.

She was thirteen.

For the first time in her life, she was out of words.

Rose worked in a hat factory with other young immigrants like her—people from Russia, Romania, Poland.

From eight in the morning until ten at night, Rose sewed linings into men's hats.

Her neck hurt.
Her eyes got tired.

Rose had to buy her own sewing machine. All the workers did.

Rose carried it to work each morning.

"Faster, faster, faster!" the bosses would yell.

Rose would sew faster.

She kept her mouth shut.

Her family needed the money.

After a while, though, Rose got tired of the dirt and the cold and the rats at the factory.

Then, her friend told her that women workers were earning less money than men.

Rose got mad.

The shop should be clean. It should be fair.
Rose wanted to speak out.

Words started filling her up again.

Rose thought if the workers spoke out together their voices would be louder.

Rose talked with other women workers.

She wanted them—together—
to ask the owner to get rid of
the rats in the factory, and to
provide clean water to drink
during the day.

And to pay them more money,
equal to the men.

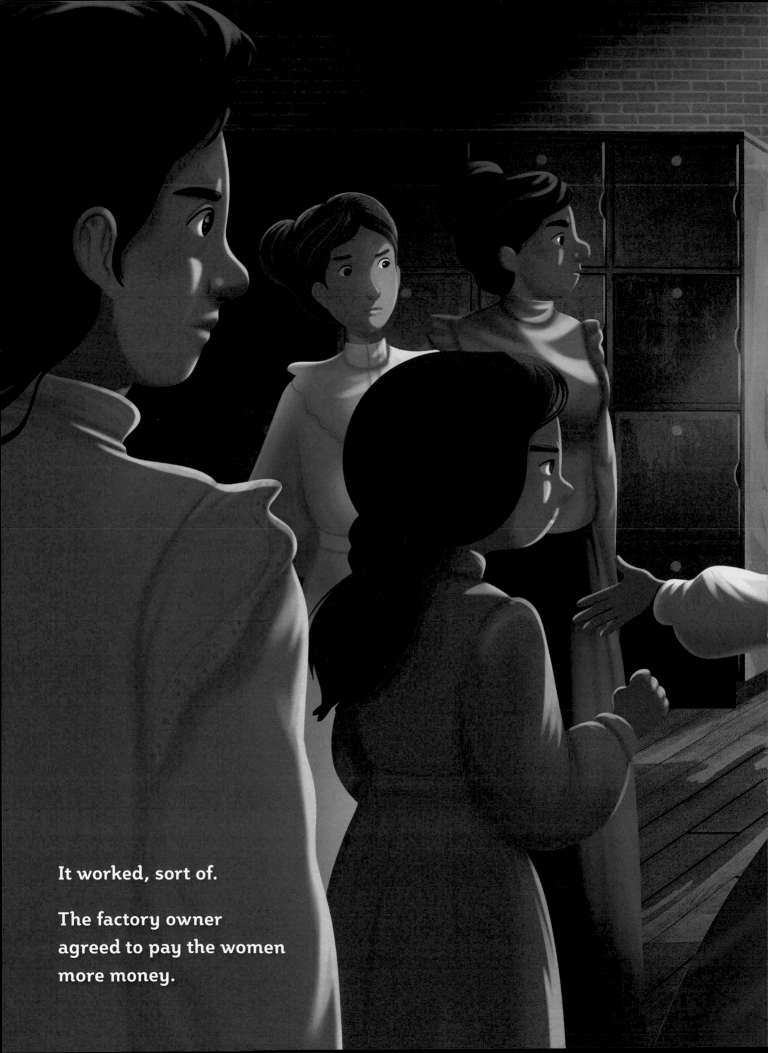

It worked, sort of.

The factory owner agreed to pay the women more money.

Rose and her friends were happy to finally get paid a fairer wage.

But the factory stayed dirty and cold and unsafe.

In New York City at that time, there were many, many other factories that didn't treat workers fairly.

The factories were squished together, up and down the streets.

Rose wanted ALL the factories
to be fairer.

Rose stood on a ladder on the street and made speeches.

Workers from many factories crowded around and listened to the small young woman with the big loud voice.

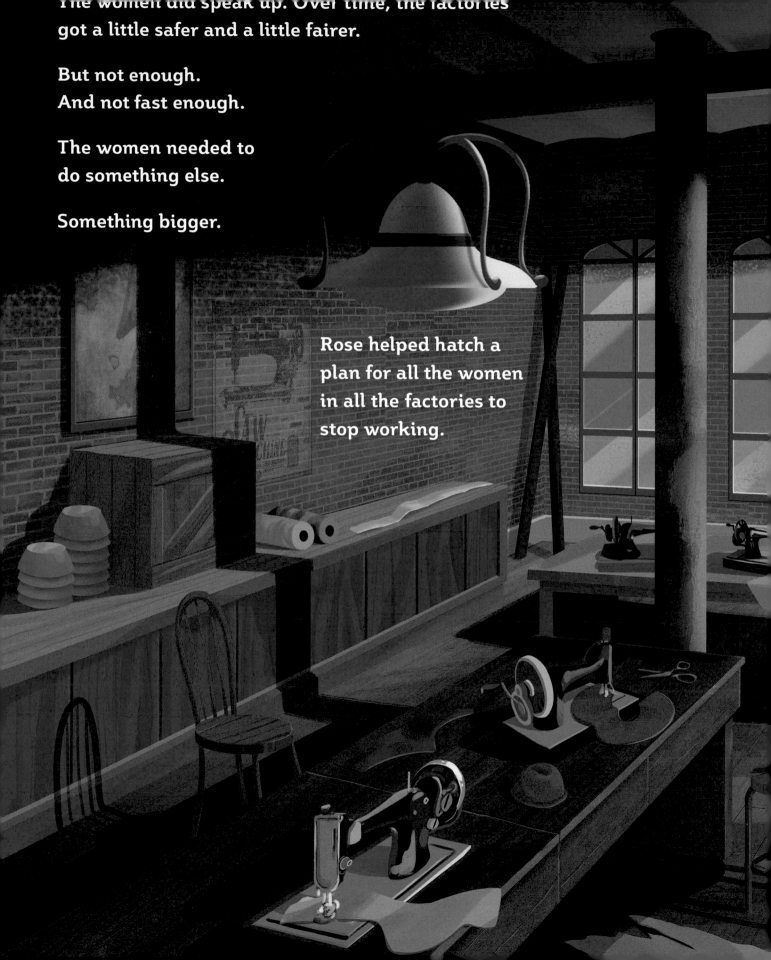

The women did speak up. Over time, the factories got a little safer and a little fairer.

But not enough.
And not fast enough.

The women needed to do something else.

Something bigger.

Rose helped hatch a plan for all the women in all the factories to stop working.

They would not come back until they got what they were asking for.

One cold November day in 1909, it was time to act.

All of them. All at once.

Rose turned off her sewing machine, stood up, and walked out.

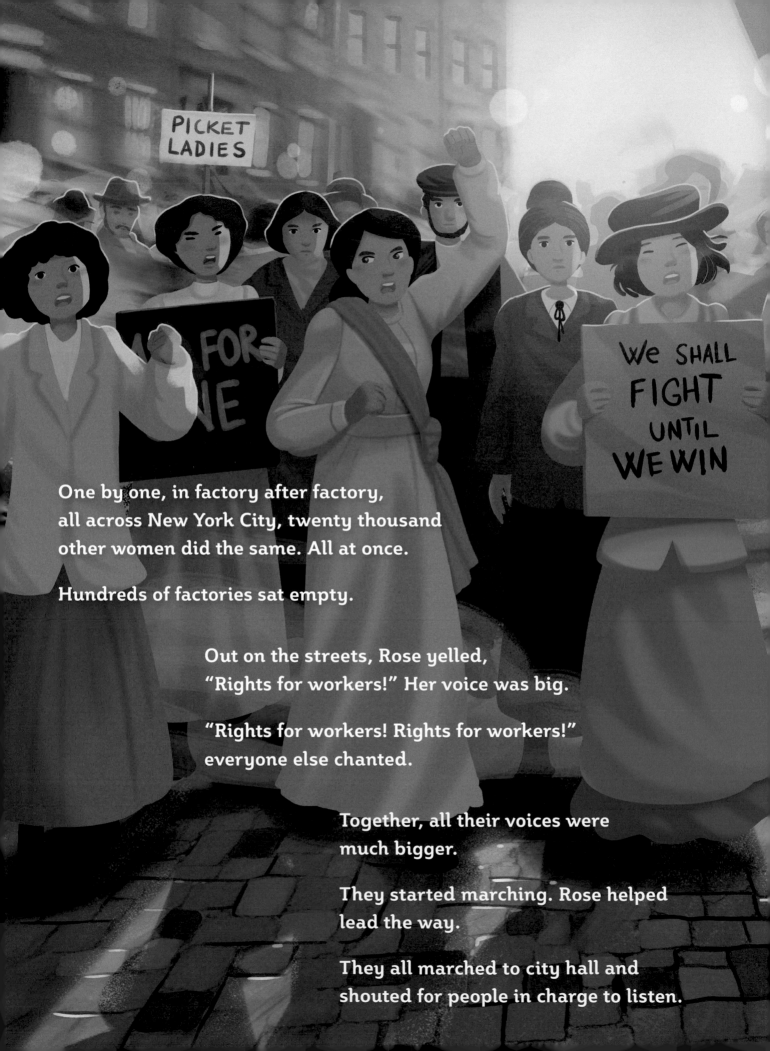

One by one, in factory after factory, all across New York City, twenty thousand other women did the same. All at once.

Hundreds of factories sat empty.

Out on the streets, Rose yelled, "Rights for workers!" Her voice was big.

"Rights for workers! Rights for workers!" everyone else chanted.

Together, all their voices were much bigger.

They started marching. Rose helped lead the way.

They all marched to city hall and shouted for people in charge to listen.

The people in charge did listen, sort of.

Some factories became a little fairer.

The workers didn't have to buy their own tools and sewing machines anymore.

But some factories still weren't safe.

Two years after that strike:

Fire! Fire!

The doors at the Triangle Shirtwaist Company were locked when a fire began inside.

One hundred and forty-six workers could not get out, and they died.

Rose and her friends stood silently while the enormous funeral passed by.

They were very angry.

They had asked and shouted and marched for safety and fairness.

Some things had changed.
But not enough.

Rose could feel the anger
inside herself.

She could feel everyone's anger.

Her words were growing stronger,
waiting to erupt.

Thousands of people crowded into the
Metropolitan Opera House—poor workers
from downtown, rich people from uptown.

Everyone was together.
People shouted different ideas.
But they could not agree on
what to do to keep workers safe.

Rose climbed the steps to
the stage and faced the crowd.

But for the first time,
words stuck in her throat.

She'd never spoken in
front of so many rich and
powerful people before.

Rose started slowly, her voice growing louder and stronger with each word.

"Too much blood has been spilled. I know from experience that it is up to the working people to save themselves"

Everyone stopped arguing.

The workers listened. The rich people listened.

The newspaper reporters listened and wrote about Rose's speech.

And eventually,
the people in charge
listened too.

They made new rules to keep workers safer.

For the rest of her life,
Rose spoke out for
workers' rights.

Presidents listened.
Congress listened.

Over time, all over the
United States, factories
became fairer and workers
became safer.

Because Rose spoke out.

More about Rose Schneiderman

Rose Schneiderman as a young woman, circa 1907
Source: Library of Congress

Rose Schneiderman was born in Poland in 1882. In 1890, she and her family moved to New York City, along with many other Jewish immigrants from Eastern Europe and Russia. They had experienced persecution in their homelands because of their faith and escaped to the United States in search of safety and freedom.

Despite standing only four feet nine, Rose was a woman of towering courage. She became one of the leading labor activists of her time.

In one of her most famous speeches, Rose said, "What the woman who labors wants is the right to live, not simply exist. . . . The worker must have bread, but she must have roses, too."

Rose argued that workers should have more than simply a paycheck. They deserve a full human existence, complete with beauty.

Rose worked for labor equality her entire life. She became president of the National Women's Trade Union League and an advisor to President Franklin Roosevelt. He appointed her as the only woman on the National Labor Advisory Board, and later, she became New York's secretary of labor. Throughout her lifetime, Rose led reforms that made a real difference for workers everywhere.

Dear Readers,

Rose Schneiderman was never afraid to speak out when she saw people being treated unfairly.

She was part of a long Jewish tradition of activism and pursuit of social justice. Fifty years after Rose marched in the streets of New York City for workers' rights, Rabbi Abraham Joshua Heschel walked arm in arm with Dr. Martin Luther King Jr. in 1965 in Alabama, from Selma to Montgomery, to support civil rights for Black Americans. Heschel and many other Jewish social activists were following in Rose's footsteps.

Jewish tradition teaches that we all have an obligation to work toward *tikun olam*—repairing the world. Rose understood this idea: When she saw something broken in the world around her, she worked to fix it. She wanted to make sure that everyone had an equal chance at a beautiful, happy, peaceful life.

I hope you think of Rose the next time you see injustice around you. I hope you speak out like she did.